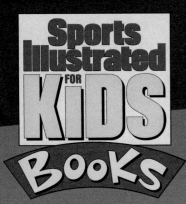

BRIAN SPURLOCK

NASCAR STARS AND CARS

BY LARS ANDERSON

CONTENTS

NIGEL KINRADE

INTRODUCTION

Welcome to the country's largest spectator sport — NASCAR. Here's what you'll find at any Winston Cup race: lanes of colorful cars driven by the world's greatest stock-car drivers. The stadiums are filled with thousands of cheering fans. No wonder three TV networks paid $400 million to broadcast NASCAR races for the next six years.

You don't only have to flip on the television to get the hottest NASCAR action. You can find it right here in **SPORTS ILLUSTRATED FOR KIDS** *NASCAR Stars and Cars.* All the thrills, chills, and excitement of stock-car racing is jam-packed in these pages. Get the inside scoop on all of NASCAR's best road-runners such as Jeff Gordon, Tony Stewart, Bobby Labonte, and Dale Jarrett.

So, are you ready? Get set, go!

3

DALE JARRETT

CAR FACTS

Make: **Ford**
Model: **Taurus**
Number: 88
Owner: **Robert Yates Racing**
Crew Chief: **Todd Parrott**

Dale Jarrett *never* gave up. There were times during his first 14 years on the NASCAR circuit when he thought about quitting, but he didn't. He kept on driving. Finally in 1999, at age 43, Dale was rewarded for his hard work and perseverance.

That's when Dale won his first Winston Cup championship. He became the second-oldest first-time series champion ever. Only Bobby Allison was older when he won the title for the first time. (Bobby did it at age 45, in 1983.)

But Dale's championship really wasn't that surprising. He finished second in the standings in 1997, and third in 1998. He had 18 career victories entering the 1999 season.

Besides, stock-car racing success runs in the family. Dale's dad, Ned, was a NASCAR champion in 1961 and 1965. Dale and Ned are the first father and son to win NASCAR's top title since Lee and Richard Petty, who joined that club in 1965!

"There were times when I'd wonder if this was exactly what I was supposed to do in life," Dale once said about the times he thought of quitting, "and what was going to happen even if I was able to *stay* in the sport — what degree of impact I might have on NASCAR."

Dale might have had a career in a completely different sport. In high school, he was a gifted golfer. "But there is no doubt that I made the right choice," says Dale. Everyone in NASCAR would agree.

TOM RAYMOND

How sweet it is! After a 14-year wait, Dale won his first NASCAR championship in 1999.

Bobby Labonte has always been known as Terry Labonte's little brother. But in 1999, Little Brother Bobby became a Big Guy on the Winston Cup circuit when he finished second in the points standings.

Bobby's greatest victory came at the Pepsi 400, in August. Over the race's final 18 laps, he outmaneuvered Jeff Gordon and Dale Earnhardt, both former Winston Cup champions, to take the checkered flag. The victory was Bobby's fourth of the season. It helped establish him as one of the best drivers in all of NASCAR.

The 1999 season was the best season of Bobby's eight-year career. Great driving skills and determination, of course, helped Bobby succeed. Another key to his improvement can be traced to Joe Gibbs, who owns Bobby's car.

Joe coached the NFL's Washington Redskins and led them to four Super Bowls. He got involved with NASCAR in 1991. When he created his NASCAR team, Joe picked Bobby to be his star player. Then he surrounded Bobby with some of the most talented crewmen in the business.

"Our goal is to finish in the top five each weekend," says crew chief Jimmy Makar. "If we can do that, week in and week out, the wins will come and we will be in the points race."

And Terry Labonte's Little Brother Bobby will continue to be a Big Guy in NASCAR.

NIGEL KINRADE

BOBBY LABONTE

Oh, brother! Bobby's breakout year gave NASCAR another Labonte star.

CAR FACTS

Make: **Pontiac**
Model: **Grand Prix**
Number: **18**
Owner: **Joe Gibbs Racing**
Crew Chief: **Jimmy Makar**

MARK MARTIN

Mark Martin is known as the toughest guy in NASCAR. And no wonder: In 1999, he wrecked his car at the Daytona 500 and suffered injuries to his back, knee, and wrist. A weaker person would have sat out the year.

But Mark shrugged off the pain and kept going. He went on to win two races and finish third in the Winston Cup point standings! It was the seventh straight year Mark finished among the Top 5 drivers in points.

Through 1999, Mark had won 31 races during his 14 seasons on the circuit. Mark had 34 career victories in the NASCAR Busch Series, which is the minor leagues of NASCAR. Most drivers start in the Busch Series before moving over to the Winston Cup circuit.

Overcoming injuries and winning on NASCAR's most difficult tracks aren't the only reasons Mark is tough. Of all the tough challenges Mark has faced, the toughest was dealing with the loss of his father. In August 1998, Julian Martin was killed when the plane he was flying crashed. Mr. Martin had taught Mark how to drive. They had been really close. Mark was heartbroken about his dad's death.

"I felt helpless," says Mark. "It was hard to think and organize."

Mark *did* get himself together. Even though he was driving with a heavy heart, he won seven times and earned more than $3 million in prize money in 1998. Mark finished second in the Winston Cup points standings that season.

Now that's tough!

Mark shrugged off injuries to finish third in the 1999 Winston Cup point standings.

CAR FACTS

Make:
Ford

Model:
Taurus

Number: **6**

Owner:
Roush Racing

Crew Chief:
Jimmy Fennig

Make: **Pontiac**
Model: **Grand Prix**
Number: **20**
Owner: **Joe Gibbs Racing**
Crew Chief: **Greg Zipadelli**

TOM RAYMOND

Tony zoomed through the season, becoming the only rookie to ever win three races.

TONY STEWART

NIGEL KINRADE

Tony Stewart was a rookie in 1999, but he drove like an old pro. In his first season on the Winston Cup circuit, Tony became the only rookie driver to ever win three races. He also finished fourth in the points standings, higher than any other first-year driver.

"Most rookies, myself included, take about fifteen races to really get comfortable and stop tearing up cars," says fellow driver Jeff Gordon. "It only took Tony . . . well, not that many."

It certainly didn't! During a 32-race span from March through November 1999, Tony had 22 Top 10 finishes. His first win came in September, when he took the checkered flag at Richmond International Raceway. No rookie had won a Winston Cup race since Davey Allison did it in 1987. In November, he became the first rookie in 37 years to win back-to-back events.

The secret to Tony's success is that he has been driving everything and anything for as long as he can remember. When he was 5, he would ride anything, from a plastic toy motorcycle to his mom's vacuum cleaner, all the while wearing a mixing bowl as a makeshift helmet. He graduated to racing go-karts at age 6 and by age 12 he was a national champ.

In 1995, Tony became the first driver to win the United States Auto Club triple crown in midgets, sprint car, and Silver Crown. In 1997, he won an Indy car race.

After one season on NASCAR's top circuit, Tony was a star. It may be just a matter of time before he wins the Winston Cup title.

JEFF BURTON

When Jeff Burton is good, he's very, very good. But when he is bad . . . well, he is really bad. Look at Jeff's 1999 performance: He drove his Ford Taurus to victory in six Winston Cup races. Jeff Gordon is the only driver who won more. (Jeff won seven.)

But Jeff also finished 35th or worse in six races. That killed his hopes of winning the Winston Cup title. You have to be consistent to win championships!

"We're proud to be winning this many races, but we're disappointed that we've finished last and 35th and 37th as many times as we have," says Jeff.

"We're disappointed in those finishes, but if we're learning things from it that we can apply to the future, it's a debt well-paid."

In seven full years on the Winston Cup circuit, Jeff has collected 11 wins, 67 Top 5 finishes, and more than $11 million in prize money. He was the 1994 Rookie of the Year.

Jeff's love for racing started at a young age. When he was five, Jeff watched his older brother, Ward, drive go-karts. Jeff was so excited that he convinced his parents to let him drive too. Since then, Jeff has been a success.

Could he win the Winston Cup? Mark Martin certainly think's he is good enough.

"Without a doubt, Jeff's the best," says Mark, Jeff's teammate. "If I were to start a racing team today, nothing could stop me from getting Jeff to be my driver."

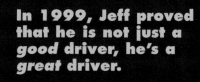

In 1999, Jeff proved that he is not just a *good* driver, he's a *great* driver.

RUISTY JARRETT/ALLSPORT

CAR FACTS

Make: **Ford**
Model: **Taurus**
Number: **99**
Owner: **Roush Racing**
Crew Chief: **Frank Stoddard**

GEORGE TIEDEMANN

Dale Earnhardt has been driving race cars since 1975. He has won more than 60 Winston Cup races. But it isn't his victories that keep people talking about Dale. It's the rough and rugged way he drives. He is such a warrior that he has earned the nickname "the Intimidator."

In 1980, the Intimidator became the first driver to win the Winston Cup points championship the year after winning the Rookie of the Year award. Dale won his second points title in 1986 and took it again in 1987, when he won 11 of 29 races.

As the years went on, Dale became even tougher. From 1990 to 1994, he collected four more Winston Cup championships, for a grand total of seven. Only the legendary Richard Petty has won as many Winston Cup titles!

In 1999, Dale proved that at the age of 50, he's still as intimidating as ever. During the final lap of the Goody's Headache Powder 500, Dale bumped Terry Labonte into a wall to pass him. Dale then won the race.

"There is one word to describe Dale — *determination*," says Richard Childress, the owner of Dale's race team. "He is driven by competition and to do his best at every race. That is the reason he is where he is today."

Where is Dale? He's tailgating his way to a very short list of the greatest NASCAR drivers of all time.

GEORGE TIEDEMANN

GEORGE TIEDEMANN

DALE EARNHARDT

CAR FACTS

Make:
Chevrolet
Model:
Monte Carlo
Number: **3**
Owner:
Richard Childress
Crew Chief:
Kevin Hamlin

Dale's rugged driving has earned him more than 60 victories.

JEFF GORDON

CAR FACTS

Make: Chevrolet
Model: Monte Carlo
Number: 24
Owner: Hendrick Motorsports
Crew Chief: Brian Whitesell

Jeff Gordon is the golden boy of NASCAR. Through 1999, when he turned 28 years old, he had already won three championships, 49 races, and more than $26 million in prize money! Barring any major detours, he was well on the road to becoming a legend.

"He's not just the driver of the future, he's the driver of the immediate future," fellow driver Dale Jarrett said. "He's going to be a pain in our sides for a long time." Those words were true in 1999 and apply to 2000, but Dale said them in 1993! Two years later, in 1995, Jeff became the youngest person in 45 years to win the Winston Cup Series title. He was 24. (Bill Rexford won the title at age 23 in 1950.)

Jeff has been racing almost as long as he has been walking. When he was 5 years old, his stepfather bought him two quarter-midget race cars. When he was 8 years old, he won the U.S. quarter-midget championship. By the time he was 14, his family had moved from their home in California to Pitsboro, Indiana, just so that Jeff could compete in more car races. That move paid off big for Jeff.

In 1993, Jeff was named Winston Cup Rookie of the Year. He also earned the nickname Wonder Boy that season. It's a name NASCAR fans probably will be calling him for a long, long time.

By age 28, Jeff had already won 49 races. No wonder he is called Wonder Boy!

BRIAN SPURLOCK

Rusty Wallace was a goner. That's what the fans watching from the stands of Bristol International Raceway, in Bristol, Tennessee, thought.

Rusty was taking a practice run for the 1988 Busch 500 race when suddenly he blew a tire. His car turned over on its side six times down the front straightaway as the fans watched in horror. When rescue workers reached the car, Rusty wasn't breathing.

After being worked on by paramedics, Rusty started breathing. Rusty not only survived, he came back to race the very next day! The accident didn't slow Rusty down one bit. That year, he finished second in the Winston Cup points race. The next year, he won the NASCAR championship.

"I'm an impatient person," says Rusty. "It's why I could never be a hot-air balloonist."

Rusty was off to a blazing start the moment he joined the Winston Cup circuit, in 1980. He was named Rookie of the Year in 1984 and has remained one of the best drivers on the circuit. Through 1999, Rusty won at least one race in 14 straight seasons. He had also finished in the Top 10 an amazing 53 percent of the time.

"When the history book of the modern era of NASCAR racing is written," says Rusty, "I want to be remembered as a top competitor."

No problem, Rusty.

Away he goes! **Rusty keeps roaring past his competition.**

GEORGE TIEDEMANN

RUSTY WALLACE

CAR FACTS

Make:
Ford
Model:
Taurus
Number: **2**
Owner:
Penske South Racing
Crew Chief:
Robin Pemberton

No one had ever heard of Mike Skinner. When he burst onto the NASCAR scene, in 1997, even racing veterans had no idea where he had come from.

That's because Mike had spent the first 20 years of his career racing on some of NASCAR's smaller tracks in Nevada and California. Mike had dominated those races — but had not made much money. So his wife, Beth, told him to either pursue a racing career full-time or quit talking about it. Mike decided to go for it.

He quickly moved through the various levels of stock cars, zooming onto the Winston Cup circuit in two full seasons. In 1997, Mike fulfilled a childhood dream of being named the Winston Cup Rookie of the Year! He posted three Top 10 finishes and won more than $900,000.

Mike's race to the top continued, as he climbed up the NASCAR ladder a few notches each year. In his first season on the Winston Cup circuit, Mike finished 30th in the points standings. In his second season, he finished 21st, and in 1999, he finished in 10th place.

But Mike still had one big goal ahead of him: He had yet to win a Winston Cup race. Whenever he does win one, no one will be surprised. Racing fans know who Mike Skinner is now: He's a very talented driver!

TOM RAYMOND

GEORGE TIEDEMANN

MIKE SKINNER

CAR FACTS

Make: **Chevrolet**
Model: **Monte Carlo**
Number: **31**
Owner: **Richard Childress**
Crew Chief: **Larry McReynolds**

Mike's third season was a good one: He finished 10th in points.

Watch out, guys, I'm here! That's what Ward Burton told NASCAR drivers with his 1999 Winston Cup performance. Ward didn't win a race, but he proved that he can and will, be a contender. In 1999, Ward finished in the Top 10 in a race 15 times — the most ever in his career — and ended the season in ninth place in the points standings.

"Everything about Winston Cup racing is about winning, but to me there's not a lot of difference between saying 'We won this race' versus 'We're having a winning year,'" Ward said. "Well, we had a winning year, and we got better each week."

It was a nice improvement over the previous year, even if Ward did finish behind his younger brother, Jeff, in the standings. *(Read more about Jeff on page 12.)* In 1998, Ward finished in 16th place and earned more than $1.3 million in prize money. In 1999, he won $2 million, thanks to all those Top 10 finishes. Even better, Ward went no more than two races all season between Top 10 runs. The only other drivers to accomplish that were Dale Jarrett, Bobby Labonte, Mark Martin, Jeff Gordon, and Dale Earnhardt. That's good company!

Wade has remained just a few steps behind his brother. But Jeff thinks that may change. "My brother is going to win the whole darn thing one of these days," Jeff says. "I'm sure he will."

GEORGE TIEDEMANN

Ward's Cat car often led the pack in 1999.

WARD BURTON

NIGEL KINRADE

TERRY LABONTE

CAR FACTS

Make: **Chevrolet**
Model: **Monte Carlo**
Number: **5**
Owner: **Hendrick Motorsports**
Crew Chief: **Andy Graves**

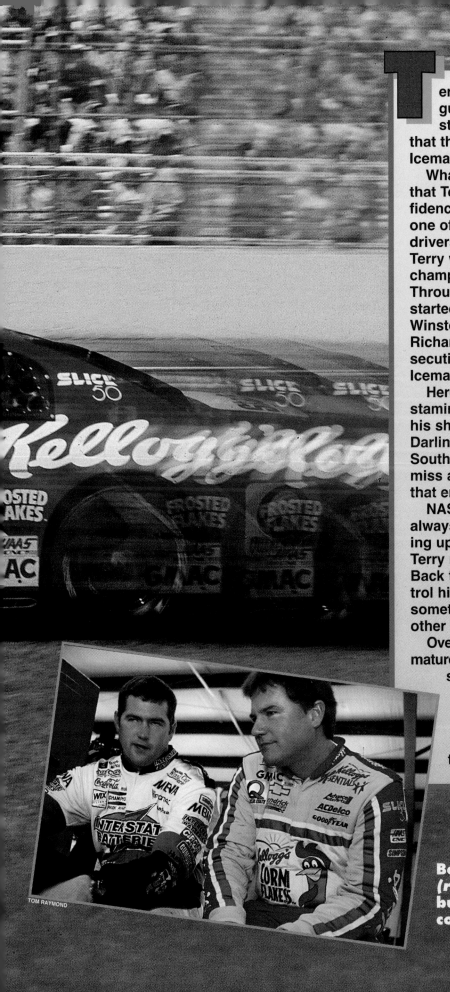

Terry Labonte is the coolest guy in NASCAR. He is so steady and so sure of himself that the other drivers call him Iceman. That's cool!

What's *really* cool, though, is that Terry has used that cool confidence on the track to become one of the most successful drivers in Winston Cup history. Terry won the Winston Cup points championships in 1984 and 1996. Through the 1999 season, he had started a record 638 consecutive Winston Cup races. (Terry broke Richard Petty's record of 513 consecutive starts in April 1996.) The Iceman is also an iron man.

Here's one story about Terry's stamina: In April 1987, he broke his shoulder in a wreck at Darlington Raceway, in Darlington, South Carolina. But Terry didn't miss a race — not a single race! — that entire season.

NASCAR's iron man wasn't always an Iceman. As a kid growing up in Corpus Christi, Texas, Terry raced quarter-midget cars. Back then, he did not always control his emotions. Terry would sometimes get into fights with other drivers.

Over the years, Terry has matured. He has become one of the steadiest guys around. For good reason.

"It takes the same thing to win now as it did in 1984," says Terry. "You have to be consistent."

TOM RAYMOND

Bobby (*left*) and Terry (*right*) are brothers, but they are fierce competitors.

NIGEL KINRADE

Kyle Petty grew up in one of the greatest racing dynasties in NASCAR history. His grandfather Lee Petty won the Daytona 500 in 1959. Lee's son, Richard, won more races (200) than any other driver in NASCAR history. What career did Kyle choose? He decided to follow in his father's and grandfather's footsteps and race cars for a living.

At age 19, Kyle joined the Winston Cup series. He became one of the most popular drivers around. NASCAR fans love seeing Kyle streak around the tracks in his blue Hot Wheels car.

In 1992 and 1993, Kyle had some Petty-like success, too. Both years, he finished fifth in the points standings. Through 1999, though, Kyle had won only eight races in 21 years on the circuit.

But Kyle has been very successful in raising money for NASCAR charities. Every year since 1995, he takes a cross-country motorcycle trip to raise money.

Kyle has raised something else, too: Another NASCAR-driving Petty. His son, Adam, who turned 19 in 1999, will compete in five Winston Cup races in 2000 and plans to join the circuit full-time in 2001. When Adam makes his Winston Cup debut, he will become the only fourth-generation athlete to compete full-time in any major sports organization.

Kyle's Hot Wheels car has made him one of NASCAR's most popular drivers.

DAVID TAYLOR—ALLSPORT

KYLE PETTY

DARRELL WALTRIP

CAR FACTS

Make:
Ford
Model:
Taurus
Number: 66
Owner: **Travis Carter Motorsports**
Crew Chief: **Travis Carter**

During his 28-year career on the Winston Cup circuit, Darrell Waltrip was known as a smooth talker who never had trouble getting the words out. Never, that is, until he announced his retirement from the sport in August 1999.

That day, he had to choke back tears and struggle to complete a sentence. "I've done this for many years," said Darrell. "We've gotten up every morning, put on our racing gear, and gone to the track. In sports, your legs and arms give out. One thing that never gives out is the heart. It's the things that carry it around that have given out."

Darrell's heart helped him become a NASCAR legend. He earned three Winston Cup titles, in 1981, 1982, and 1985. He won 12 races in each of his first two championship seasons. Darrell won the Daytona 500 in 1989. He's also the only three-time winner of the United States Auto Club American Driver of the Year award. He won that in 1979, 1981, and 1982. All told, Darrell won 84 Winston Cup races, which ties him for third place on the all-time Winston Cup win list.

Darrell, 52, traces his success to the go-kart races he ran as a kid in a supermarket parking lot.

"There's nothing quite like a go-kart to teach you the fundamentals of racing," he says. "It taught me everything I needed to know."

When Darrell retired, in 1999, a NASCAR legend left the track.

GEORGE TIEDEMANN

JEREMY MAYFIELD

CAR FACTS

Make:
Ford
Model:
Taurus
Number: **12**
Owner: **Penske-Kranefuss Racing**
Crew Chief:
Peter Sospenzo

GEORGE TIEDEMANN (2)

Jeremy has worked hard to become one of the top drivers on the NASCAR circuit.

When Jeremy Mayfield was in high school in Owensboro, Kentucky, he wasn't like most teenagers. He didn't spend time hanging out with his friends at the mall or going to the movies. Jeremy spent all *his* free time at the garage, working on cars.

"I just knew what I wanted to do, knew what I wanted to be," says Jeremy. "I loved racing and that's all I did, every day, every night. On the weekends, everybody else was doing his own deal. I was racing."

Jeremy still spends all his weekends racing — only now it's on the top stock-car racetracks in the world!

Jeremy joined the Winston Cup circuit in 1994 and finished 34th in the standings as a rookie. In 1998, he finished in the top five in eight of the first 16 races and had the Winston Cup points lead for much of May and June. He finished in seventh place for the year. In 1999, he finished in 11th place in the points standings.

As much time as Jeremy has spent working on cars and racing them, he knows he has to spend even more time in order to become a great driver.

"Racing isn't easy," says Jeremy. "You have to work all the time to get into Victory Lane." Good thing for Jeremy, there's nothing he'd rather do.

LAST MILE

There are many flags at NASCAR races, but there is only one flag every driver wants: the checkered flag.

TOM RAYMOND